DNA and Gen
Simplified

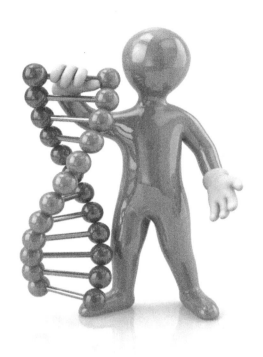

By Stephen Szabados

DNA and Genealogy Research: Simplified

DEDICATION

For my children and my grandsons - my genealogy research
is made more important because of them

Table of Content

Introduction

The DNA testing companies have flooded the market with many promotional ads that promise to unlock secrets in our family trees. The result of the promotions has generated large sales of DNA test kits and large numbers of genealogists who are looking for methods to understand their DNA test results. I hope this book will give the reader some hints on how to use your DNA test results to expand your genealogical research and your family history.

Sample Promotion from FamilyTreeDNA (Aug. 2019)

SUMMER SALE

Summer savings on Family Finder, Y-DNA, and mtDNA

$20 to $150 off select tests

SHOP NOW

Begin Your
DNA Journey
Swab Collection Kit

FamilyTreeDNA

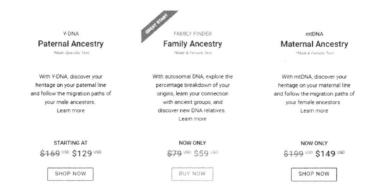

Y-DNA	FAMILY FINDER	mtDNA
Paternal Ancestry	GREAT START **Family Ancestry**	**Maternal Ancestry**
Male-Specific Test	*Male & Female Test*	*Male & Female Test*
With Y-DNA, discover your heritage on your paternal line and follow the migration paths of your male ancestors. Learn more	With autosomal DNA, explore the percentage breakdown of your origins, learn your connection with ancient groups, and discover new DNA relatives. Learn more	With mtDNA, discover your heritage on your maternal line and follow the migration paths of your female ancestors Learn more
STARTING AT	NOW ONLY	NOW ONLY
$169 USD $129 USD	$79 USD $59 USD	$199 USD $149 USD
SHOP NOW	BUY NOW	SHOP NOW

I am not a medical doctor nor a genetic scientist. I will try to explain using DNA in genealogy research employing using non-scientific terms. And therefore, I will not discuss Chromosome browsers, haplogroups, or SNPs in this book.

I will explain how to use the basic tools supplied by the DNA testing companies to understand your DNA results better. I will try to stick to the basics and therefore, not discuss the advanced tools or third-party tools at this time. The critical value of this book is my explanation of how to overcome the scientific nature of the tests by looking at your results using traditional genealogical skills. My explanation includes practical examples of how to use the tools, and my goal is to simplify how you analyze your results in terms that all of us as genealogist can understand. I present a case study in Chapter Three, where I discuss using these tools to find a biological father whose existence was a total surprise to his son.

Researchers are seeking answers to these questions:
- Understanding what their DNA results mean? Ethnicity, relationships, etc.
- How are they related to the people who show up as their DNA matches?
- Can these cousins help fill in the blanks in the family tree?
- Do they need to identify everyone that shows up as DNA matches? (How deep should they go?)

In most cases, the results of the tests have delivered no surprises and may seem boring. In some cases, DNA results produced significant clues and knocked down brick walls. However, many cases do not match the family tree created from the paper trail and have caused confusion with the test takers. It is not an easy science to understand, and many test-takers are confused by the results they see.

- What tools do the DNA testing companies supply?
- What third-party software is available?
- What books are available?
- What educational opportunities are available?
- Is there an expert that can help?

I purposely avoid discussing the complex science of DNA and the use of third-party software because I believe we can answer most of our questions about our DNA results by using the simple tools the major companies (AncestryDNA, FamilyTreeDNA (FTDNA), and MyHeritageDNA) provide on their websites. Using these tools require the same expertise and logic as our basic genealogy research skills.

The material will cover:
- Why genealogists take DNA tests
- Give a brief description of types of DNA tests
- List the benefits of each type of DNA test
- Show examples of the results offered from DNA testing
- Compare the major DNA testing companies
- Discuss how to use the tools to understand your DNA results
- Review, one case study, showing how the basic tools helped find a previously unknown relative.
- Review the emotional concerns dealing with problematic results

Use the material you find in this book to better understand your results. Use the tools discussed in this book to find the clues in your DNA results that will allow you to gain more information and insight about your family history. Genealogy can be an addiction, so do not let DNA results be your only genealogy focus. Review the goals you had when you ordered your test kit and keep your focus on your long-term genealogical goals.

Review the material carefully as I show that DNA testing is only one tool in our genealogy tool kit. It is a powerful tool but uses it wisely. Learn to use DNA test data and traditional genealogical techniques in tandem, and you will be able to harness the full value of genetic testing.

Chapter One - DNA Testing

DNA seems to be taking over genealogy research by storm, and we should start considering genetic genealogy an essential tool for our family history research.

However, you will find that your DNA results will not magically fill out your family tree. DNA testing is just one tool in the genealogist's toolbox. To be successful, you need to use your test results with personal and historical records and stories to compile a complete picture of family and personal relationships. Your test results cannot answer every family history question. However, your results may give you clues to where to look for more information, and when used with traditional research, it becomes a powerful tool that can help you expand your family history.

- If you have a brick wall, DNA may point you to a solution, especially in areas where records have been lost or destroyed.
- Your results may also give you insights as to the origins of your ancestors and identify general areas where you can find records.
- You may also meet new cousins or reconnect with known cousins, and they may fill in some of the unknown branches of your family tree.

You must remember that you still have to do the essential work. DNA testing is only a tool and not a magic wand.

Scientists began developing methods to sequence (or quantify) our DNA in the early 1970s and were able to sequence human DNA in 1984 for the first time fully. Scientists used it as a tool to accelerate biological and medical research. Genealogist saw the benefit of this discovery in 1997 when GeneTree began providing Y-DNA and mtDNA test kits to the public. In 2000, FamilyTreeDNA (FTDNA) started offering Y-DNA and mtDNA test kits to the public. Ancestry.com also began offering Y-DNA and mtDNA test kits after 2000 to the public, but they decided discontinued offering these tests in 2014 and began offering autosomal test kits only.

In 2005, National Geographic Society launched a genetic study to map historical human migration patterns using their Geno 2.0 testing and switched to autosomal (atDNA) in 2009. The Society ended the public participation in this project on May 31, 2019, and they plan to maintain the website where customers can access their results only through December 31, 2020.[1]

The use of DNA in genealogy research exploded when 23andMe started offering autosomal DNA test kits in 2007. AncestryDNA and Family Tree DNA quickly followed 23andMe and began offering autosomal kits. 23andMe was new to offering DNA testing to genealogists and accelerated their growth by having regular discounted sales of their test kits. The other testing companies followed 23andMe and ran numerous discounted sales of their kits. This competition continues today. AncestryDNA and 23andMe had processed over one million test kits and have continued to increase their databases as they sell thousands of test kits each month. Now, I see TV advertising for the promotion of sales of autosomal test kits almost daily.

---

[1] Announcement about ending public participation and continuing access to customer data found on their website, June 3, 2019
https://genographic.nationalgeographic.com/

The advertised promotions usually refer to the autosomal DNA test, which is one of three available tests. FTDNA still offers Y-DNA and mitochondrial (mtDNA) test kits, and they continue to sell tests kits for Y-DNA and mtDNA because genealogy researchers use each type of test for different purposes. Autosomal seems to be the most popular, and I believe many people are taking the autosomal test to find or confirm their ethnicity. However, another reason people consider taking an atDNA test is the projected cousin matches that may give you contacts to exchange genealogical information.

Genealogists, who I talked to, gave me the following list of reasons why they submitted DNA samples:
- They were curious about their origins and ancient ancestry.
- They were hoping to find matches and possible distant relatives to exchange information.
- They doubted their paper trail and wanted to prove or disprove their oral history.
- They wanted to test relationship theories.
- Some also wanted to check for projected medical problems.

The power of genetic genealogy continues to grow as the databases of test results grow, which leads to the development of new tools and discoveries.

DNA Basics

Before proceeding, I want to review some of the basics of DNA.

Our DNA consists of 22 pairs of autosomal chromosomes. The 23rd pair are sex chromosomes (YDNA and XDNA). Males have an X and a Y chromosome. They received the Y chromosome from their fathers and the X chromosome from their mothers. Females have two X chromosomes which they received from each parent. The 23 pairs of chromosomes contain markers that give us many of our physical characteristics, mannerisms, and inherited medical risks. The final element that makes up our DNA are the rings of mitochondrial DNA (mtDNA), and mothers pass their mitochondrial DNA along to all of their children - male and female.

We inherited our mixture of DNA markers from our parents, and through them, we receive some of the DNA of our grandparents and our many generations of ancestors. We received 50% of our DNA from each parent, but the amount of grandparent DNA that was passed along from our parents was random and will probably not be 25% from each grandparent. However, the percentage from one pair of grandparents will total 50%. The randomness of the DNA explains why siblings will not have precisely the same DNA. The random selection of DNA to be passed along also cause amounts of DNA markers for each ancestor to disappear with each generation. In some cases, the autosomal DNA for distant ancestors may have disappeared entirely.

4

Types of DNA Tests:

In the following pages, I will discuss YDNA, mtDNA, and Autosomal DNA (atDNA) testing; looking at their general description, benefits, and limitations.

Y-DNA

The Y chromosome is found only in males. Sons receive it from their fathers, and therefore, only male members of the family can take the Y-DNA test. Female researchers need to have their brothers or uncles take the Y-DNA test to research their father's DNA. Male members of the family with the same Y-DNA should have the same surname unless one of the paternal ancestors changed the family surname at some point or the biological father is not named. Test results may show a close Y-DNA match, but finding the specific name of the most recent common ancestor (MRCA) may require research that goes back many generations.

Finding a close match should confirm the surname of the MRCA and will confirm or refute relationships. It would be hard to do this using only historical documents. We may get another significant benefit in a match if our match knows where their immigrant family left. The location could lead to finding more confirming information such as the names of other family members or historical records.

The main benefit of a Y-DNA test is to confirm relationships in the paternal line in distant generations. Examples of this are:

- Confirm the name the father of a distant great-grandfather using a sample from a branch of the unknown father and sample from a known descendant of the suspected father.

- Find an estimate of the surname of the unknown biological father. This change could be due to adoption or another unknown event.

My only Y-DNA match had ancestors who left the Rhine River Valley about 1750, which was confusing when compared to my previous genealogy research. My paper research indicated my paternal line should have Hungarian ancestors. Once I had other relatives take a Y-DNA test and autosomal tests, I identified that I did have German roots. My previously confusing Y-DNA match gave me a possible surname for my new paternal line.

FTDNA offers four levels of Y-DNA testing. It provides test kits that measure 37 markers, 67 markers, 111 markers, and 700 markers (Big Y Test). Testing a larger sample of markers will give a higher level of specificity when you find a match. However, if your match paid for a test at a lower number of markers, the comparison is based only on the lower level. You can order more markers to analyze by paying the upcharge for the larger test, but you need your matches to also pay for the larger test analysis to gain the benefits from the larger test. The test kit has two test samples, and the FTDNA lab can use the second test sample to do the additional test.

Y-DNA Benefits
- You share a common ancestor with your matches in your paternal line.
- Matches would reveal the birth father's surname or variation unless someone in the direct paternal line changed their surname.

Y-DNA Limitations
- Only males can take a Y-DNA test.
- Matches can come from only a small portion of the family tree
- Common ancestors may have lived hundreds of years ago and are hard to identify and validate.
- The number of generations to your most recent common ancestor can only be estimated.

The boxes indicate the ancestors in the Paternal Line

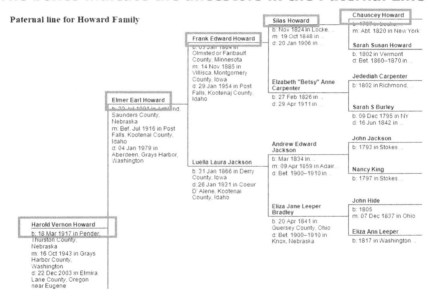

Paternal line for Howard Family

On the next page is an example of Y-DNA results showing only one match. The genetic distance of 2 indicates that not all of the 37 markers matched, and the total value of the difference was two. The name provided by the test-taker of the most distant ancestor for the match was the immigrant.

Example of Y-DNA Results

Example of comparing Y-DNA Results of matches

Marker	DYS393	DYS390	DYS19	DYS391	DYS385	DYS426	DYS388	DYS439	DYS389I	DYS392	DYS389II
SAM	13	25	13	10	13-16	12	12	12	14	13	31
HANK	13	25	13	10	13-16	12	12	12	14	13	31

Marker	DYS458	DYS459	DYS455	DYS454	DYS447	DYS437	DYS448	DYS449	DYS464
SAM	19	9-9	11	11	17	14	19	31	13-15-15-16
HANK	19	9-9	11	11	17	14	19	30	13-15-15-16

Marker	DYS460	Y-GATA-H4	YCAII	DYS456	DYS607	DYS576	DYS570	CDY	DYS442	DYS438
SAM	10	11	20-22	15	16	18	18	37-37	12	11
HANK	10	11	20-22	15	16	18	18	37-38	12	11

Note that the chart above indicates the results have only two markers out of 37 markers that do not match. The mutations are on DYS449 and CDY at a distance of one each or a total of two.

The next chart indicates that matching on 35 of 37 markers predicts the Most Recent Common Ancestor (MRCA) is within 8.4 generations with 50% probability, 16.6 generations with 90% probability, and 19.6 generations with 95% probability.

The probabilities that Hank and Sam's MRCA are:
- 7th great-grandparents are 50%
- 15th great-grandparents are 90%
- 18th great-grandparents are 95%

Most Recent Common Ancestor (MRCA) Calculator Chart[2]

Most Recent Common Ancestor Calculator		
Number of y-chromosome markers:	37	Based on the Infinite Alleles Model. Note that this model underestimates the time to MRCA. This is relatively insignificant as sample markers increase beyond 25 but can be significant with fewer markers.
Average Mutation Rate:	.0045	Please enter the number of markers and the mutation rate. Current studies suggest a mutation rate of .0043. Results will include up to 5 mismatches. More mismatches than this are probably not useful for most genealogical purposes.

Generations to MRCA vs Probability		Probability vs Generations to MRCA

	Generations to MRCA					
	37 of 37	36 of 37	35 of 37	34 of 37	33 of 37	32 of 37
Probability of Relationship %						
	Matches	Matches	Matches	Matches	Matches	Matches
25	1	3.1	5.5	8.1	10.9	13.8
30	1.2	3.5	6.1	8.8	11.7	14.7
35	1.4	3.9	6.6	9.5	12.6	15.7
40	1.7	4.3	7.2	10.2	13.3	16.6
45	1.9	4.8	7.8	10.9	14.2	17.5
50	2.2	5.3	8.4	11.7	15	18.5
55	2.5	5.8	9.1	12.4	15.9	19.4
60	2.9	6.3	9.7	13.2	16.8	20.5
65	3.3	6.9	10.5	14.1	17.8	21.6
70	3.8	7.6	11.3	15.1	18.9	22.8
75	4.3	8.3	12.3	16.2	20.1	24.1
80	5	9.3	13.4	17.4	21.5	25.7
85	5.8	10.4	14.7	19	23.3	27.6
90	7.1	12	16.6	21.1	25.6	30.1
95	9.1	14.6	19.6	24.4	29.3	34.1

Sam's ancestor, who immigrated in 1770 was his 4th great-grandfather. Hank's immigrant ancestor was his 5th great-grandfather who arrived in 1754. This example shows the difficulty of finding the paper trail to identify the MRCA for Sam and Hank due to the need to research many generations. However, this also shows the power because it points to a possible location where Sam may search for his ancestors.

---

[2] This calculator is based on the Infinite Alleles Model as described in Estimating the Time to the Most Recent Common Ancestor for the Y chromosome or Mitochondrial DNA for a Pair of Individuals, by Bruce Walsh, Department of Ecology and Evolutionary Biology, University of Arizona, published June 2001 by the Genetics Society of America.

MtDNA

MtDNA is similar in use as Y-DNA, except that this set of mitochondria is passed down from mother to her sons and daughters. It also can confirm that you and a match have a common ancestor except the relationship follows the maternal line of direct female ancestors.

The boxes indicate the ancestors in the Maternal Line

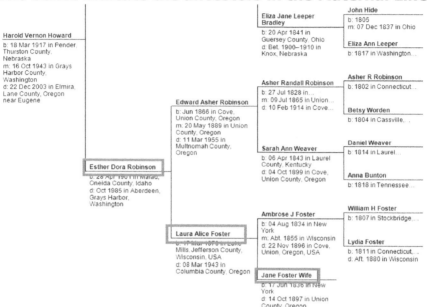

FTDNA is the only major company offering mtDNA, and it provides test kits at two levels. The lowest cost test sample (mtDNA+) analyzes the DNA in the first two regions (HVR1 and HVR2) of mtDNA and identifies basic haplogroup and migration paths. The second kit (mtDNA Full Sequencing) measures all three regions of mtDNA (HVR1, HVR2, and the coding region). FTDNA recommends the Full Sequence test for genealogical research.

Mitochondrial DNA - Benefits
- The value would be in identifying possible relationships in incomplete branches in the maternal line.
- Your close matches share a common maternal line ancestor with you

Mitochondrial DNA - Limitations
- Only checks the maternal line
- Checks only a small portion of the family tree
- Common ancestors may have lived many years ago
- The number of generations to your most recent common ancestor cannot be readily estimated

Autosomal DNA

Autosomal DNA analyzes all of your DNA, and both males and females can take the autosomal test. The testing companies give two types of results after processing the individual DNA samples: ethnicity estimates and individual DNA matches.

Ethnicity - one type of result

One set of results is the projected ethnicity, and this seems to be one of the top reasons why people are submitting DNA samples. They want to know the source of their roots. However, are these projections reliable?

Initially, some people complained that their ethnic estimates were inaccurate. In fact, the projected ethnicities are not foolproof; they are estimates based on the comparison of the test sample to a reference population used by the testing company. The companies then used their algorithms to assign to you a percentage of each ethnic group as determined by their algorithms. However, this is a relatively new science, and companies are revising their methods regularly.

The results are only an estimate and have serious limitations. Be cautious when evaluating and using your ethnicity results, especially if you are looking for clues to specific locations or countries. Use the results as clues and be patient because the results will be revised many times in the future.

On the next three pages are examples of ethnicity results from MyHeritageDNA, FamilyTreeDNA, and AncestryDNA.

⦿ MyHeritage ▷NΛ

∧ Europe		100.0%
● East Europe		50.3%
	East European	44.4%
	Balkan	5.9%
● North and West Europe		49.7%
	North and West European	34.3%
	Irish, Scottish, and Welsh	15.4%

100.0%

Example of FamilyTreeDNA Ethnic Origins Results Page

Ethnic Makeup Percentage

African	0%		Middle Eastern	0%
South Central Africa	0%		Asia Minor	0%
East Central Africa	0%		East Middle East	0%
West Africa	0%		North Africa	0%
New World	**0%**		West Middle East	0%
North and Central America ⓘ	< 1%		**European**	**99%**
South America	0%		British Isles	36%
Central/South Asian	**0%**		East Europe	63%
Central Asia	0%		Finland	0%
Oceania	0%		Scandinavia	0%
South Central Asia	0%		Southeast Europe	0%
East Asian	**0%**		Iberia	0%
Northeast Asia	0%		West and Central Europe	0%
Siberia	0%		**Jewish Diaspora**	**0%**
Southeast Asia	0%		Ashkenazi	0%
			Sephardic	0%

Example of Ancestry.com's Ethnic Origins Results Page

Ethnicity Estimate		
Eastern Europe & Russia	46%	>
England, Wales & Northwestern Europe	23%	>
Germanic Europe	12%	>
Baltic States	10%	>
Norway	6%	>
Ireland & Scotland	3%	>

I have heard some people complain that a portion of their ethnic estimates was inaccurate because it did not precisely match the paper trail. This point of view seems accurate because companies calculated these estimates using base populations, and they have recently updated their base data and improved the results. Ancestry and FTDNA recently changed my ethnic percentages, and they seem more accurate and consistent with my paper research. The companies will continue to refine their algorithms using the growing number of test samples of their new customers, and some companies are trying to find reference samples from older sources.

Two substantial factors limiting the accuracy of the ethnicity projections are the size and the specific regional populations in the reference panel. An example of how these factors affect the predictions would be when the reference population does not include a segment of the world's population, such as native Hawaiians or other groups. The ethnicity estimate cannot have that as one of the results, even if the test-taker has significant ancestry from that part of the world. Each testing company describes their reference populations in the help or information sections of their websites.

The estimated ethnicity for broad categories such as Asia, Africa, Europe, and the Americas are generally accurate, but the accuracy decreases when the projection tries to be more specific as to location or country.

There are limitations as to how much detail the projected ethnicities can show due to the widespread migrations of different people across the different continents. One example of this is the population of central and western Europe. Another example is the populations in southern Europe along the coast of the Mediterranean Sea. An example of the effect of this migration is that there are no significant differences in the DNA between Germany and France to predict which country your ancestors left accurately.

Another limitation in determining a person's ethnicity arises from the fact that the person may not have received any DNA from their ancestors from a particular region. We lose portions of DNA for older generations as each generation gets DNA from their parents. The amount of DNA from each ancestor in older generations decreases until the piece left is so small that it may not be passed along to the next generation. This scenario may eliminate DNA from a specific geographic location from our DNA.

One last significant factor confusing the results is the mysterious event that points to an unknown parent. If this happens, the ethnic estimates will not make sense, and you will not be able to confirm the projected relationships of the people matches in your list. Chapter Three will review a case study where this occurred, and a previously unknown biological father was found using the tools I will discuss in this chapter.

The testing companies continue to add DNA data from new individuals and more population segments to the reference panels. Recently, they changed many ethnic estimates that now seem more accurate. The results from the different companies still vary when compared to each other, and will likely continue to improve as they add more individual samples from more comprehensive geographical locations and sources. Eventually, I believe the projected ethnicities from each company will become closer to being similar.

Cousin Matches - the second type of result from atDNA testing

The second result of the autosomal test is a list of people who submitted a DNA sample and matched your DNA with a projected relationship to you. However, the companies do not offer guarantees of the accuracy of the relationship. The list is valuable because your matches may have information that can be added to your family history if they share the information with you. This list may also give clues to breakdown your genealogical brick walls. However, we should always confirm the relationships with genealogical methods if possible.

Companies usually quantify the closeness of the match in centimorgans matched or percentage of matched markers.

Centimorgans is a measure of length. Close relationships, such as siblings, 1st, or 2nd cousins, are usually easy to verify. However, I have found many of my projected relationships at the 4th cousin and beyond levels are challenging to confirm and typically do not produce a significant amount of useful information.

Projecting relationships from autosomal tests

- Full siblings of the same parents will share about 50% of their DNA.
- The percentage drops to 25% shared DNA with aunts, uncles, and grandparents.
- First cousins with two common grandparents share about 12.5% of their DNA
- Second cousins with two common grandparents share about 6.25% of their DNA

However, the actual percentage from a known first or second cousin may vary slightly due to the random nature of the passing of DNA from the parents to the children. We receive 50% of our DNA from each parent, but the amount of grandparent DNA that our parents pass to us will vary, and you will lose DNA from your grandparents as the passing of DNA to their children with each generation. An example of this is my sister should have 12.5% Jewish ethnicity from her great-grandfather but only has 11%. More substantial variations could also occur. As you can see from the above chart, the relationships grow more distant as the percentages decrease. As the rate drops, the more distant matches become only speculative.

The ethnic origins may match your expectations, and your close matches may be people you already know. If this is your results, DNA testing may seem boring, and you should not be confused by the results.

If your ethnic origins have a surprising ethnic origin or the matches include close matches you do not know, further research is needed to explain the results. Testing of siblings and cousins will be required to identify where the mystery began. I have found you can use the basic tools supplied by the testing company to unravel most mysteries.

Autosomal - Benefits
- This test analyzes additional autosomes (genes) not checked by mtDNA and Y-DNA tests
- The test may help discover previously unknown relatives
- The results may confirm close relationships

Autosomal - Limitations
- Some actual relationships may not show up as matches (we lose some DNA with each new generation)
- The relationships from more distant matches are only speculative
- If ancestors married cousins or were part of close-knit ethnic groups, the relationships may appear to be closer than they are.
- Use the results as clues to relationships to go around "Brick Walls."

I have heard many stories of successes in finding matches to lost branches of families that expanded family histories with many stories and pictures. However, I have also heard many people asking for help in understanding their results because they had difficulty deciphering the scientific nature of their results. To overcome the initial confusion, the testing companies introduced additional tests that dug deeper into the genetic findings, but these were scientific and required even more complicated explanations. The testing companies are now adding practical tools that help family historians better analyze and utilize their test results.

The basic tools I find useful include:
- Surname searches which review the names in your profile and family tree of your matches and displays a list that contain the surname you entered
- Identifying Shared Matches with other test subjects
- Family trees that were attached to your cousin matches
- The ability to connect notes to your matches that identify surnames and other comments that apply your relationship to your matches

All of the above tools are similar to the logic we use searching for genealogy documents. I will explain how to use them with examples in Chapter Two.

Ancestry.com has added another tool that I believe can be helpful. The new tool is Ancestry's Genetic Communities which is an analysis of large groups of test participants and identifies the general area where their ancestors left and where they settled and migrated westward in America during the different historical periods. The charts for this tool give insights about the social history of this group that may unlock some doors and a better understanding of our ancestors. I found the graphics shown for my Genetic Community made it easier to sort out how my matches are related to me.

When I finally decided to analyze the unexpected parts of my results, the new tools led me to a secret portion of my ancestry that one of my ancestors took to their grave. I am now meeting previously unknown relatives and learning fascinating new facts about my family history. However, I opened this new side of my ancestry by identifying a dark secret. So be prepared, you may also find exciting new family stories, but there may also be a dark side that you may regret discovering.

Major Testing Companies
- Family TreeDNA (FTDNA) – Y-DNA, mtDNA, and Autosomal
- 23andMe – autosomal only
- Ancestry.com – autosomal only
- MyHeritageDNA – autosomal only
- National Geographic – autosomal only (ethnic origins but no matching)
- LivingDNA – autosomal only (ethnic origins but no matching) (UK based)

In summary, I have a difficult time recommending taking a DNA test from just one company. The ethnic origins from each will differ, and I have not found tools to prove which is more accurate. I believe your ethnic origin results from each company will change over time as they refine their databases and algorithms, and your results from the different companies should become closer as DNA testing advances. Next, if your goal is to find unknown cousins, I recommend having your results in multiple databases. This strategy will compare your DNA against the largest number of other test-takers.

If multiple matches are your goal, I recommend taking the autosomal test offered by Ancestry.com and then upload the raw Ancestry DNA results onto FTDNA and MyHeritageDNA. Both companies allow free uploads that will show you more matches. To see your ethnic origins after using the free upload, FTDNA, and MyHeritageDNA, require a small fee (about $20) to add your ethnic origins.

Take Y-DNA and mtDNA tests offered by FTDNA only if you need to explore specific relationship theories. If your results are generic and match your paper trail, do not be concerned, you are probably not missing anything in your analysis of the results. If your DNA results do not match your paper trail, you may have some secrets to uncover. The other important aspect of your DNA results are the matches of your DNA to other people. If your results have matches that project as first or second cousins, contact them because you may have an exciting new source for family stories and pictures of common ancestors. However, be prepared to find aspects of your family history that you may want to forget.

My first test was a Y-DNA sample, and my purpose was an attempt to find Jewish relatives who had survived the Holocaust. I then decided to submit an autosomal sample to gain experience with this new test to answer questions during my genealogy presentations. The results from both tests did not give me the results I expected and were a source of confusion until I did further testing of relatives.

Also, please be concerned that once you identify a dark secret, you cannot ignore it or hide it. The secret is now known and becomes a part of the family history you must share. If you suspect a dark secret may exist, can you handle to answer?

Conclusions
The DNA testing companies are amassing large and growing DNA databases. However, submitting a DNA sample will not magically produce your entire family tree. Your test results may not provide any individual matches at first, but the companies run so many promotions, matches will probably show up very soon after your test. When you do have matches, you should use them as clues to possible relationships, and you should always verify these relationships with genealogical documentation. What were your goals when you submitted your DNA sample? Always

stay focused on why you want to identify these relationships.

Using DNA results, we can complete missing details and solve the mysteries of our family history. It can also help resolve problems with family memories and find distant cousins to exchange information. Our matches may help us get around a brick wall where there is no paper trail and point us in a direction that may help. The data may help you find new places to look for the documents to verify these new relationships. DNA matches may also help you jump over segments of our tree where records are lost.

If your results seem confusing, remember that scientists are still accumulating the data. The specific results that we expect may still be in development. My results were confusing and looked like "black magic." They did not match my paper trail, and my DNA matches had family trees with surnames and locations that were far from my family history. Something was very confusing with my results. They made sense only after I got more DNA test samples from relatives and collected more data and clues from traditional genealogical records such as online family trees, census records, and city directories.

Do the work; it is not magic.

Just have fun exploring your family history and heritage and remember to save and pass along what you find to your children, grandchildren, and future generations.

Chapter Two - Practical Tools to Analyze Autosomal Test Results

This chapter will discuss only Autosomal testing. It will cover how to analyze and use autosomal test results. I believe many people reacted to one of the daily TV ads and took the autosomal test to see their ethnic origins. Test-takers found that their ethnicity matched the family stories, and the results may seem boring. If a portion of your results seems wrong, you may become confused and wonder how to explain the variation. The people who submitted DNA samples to begin their genealogy research looked at their individual matches and were probably confused on how to sort through the matches to find the clues. I recommend that we need to do basic genealogy before we do DNA testing because we need to know a few generations of our family tree to be able to identify some of our close DNAA matches.

Why did you submit your DNA sample? Do you understand the results? The strategy and starting point to analyze your DNA results depend on the type of test and the goal you had when you took the test.

The Autosomal test is the most popular kit because of the price and the promise to unlock your family history. Many new test-takers are paying for this test because ads lured them with the promise of learning the ethnic origins of their ancestors. However, by looking at only the ethnic results, you are ignoring an exciting source of family information that is available from the people matches that are the second set of results produced from your DNA test. It is a versatile DNA test because it analyzes all of our DNA to show our ethnic origins, projects, close relationships, and it may find lost relatives. Go beyond the ethnic origins test results and look at your projected relatives. What information do they have that you are missing? How do you find out?

I have heard many stories of successes in finding matches to lost branches of families that expanded family histories with many stories and pictures. However, I have also heard many people asking for help in understanding their results because they had difficulty deciphering the scientific nature of their results and explained. To overcome the initial confusion, the testing companies introduced additional tests that dug deeper into the genetic findings, but these were scientific and required even more complicated explanations. The testing companies are now adding practical tools that help family historians better analyze and utilize their test results.

In this chapter, I explain how to use the basic tools that are offered by the test companies to help understand your results. I hope to keep my explanations simple and avoid discussing Haplogroups, Chromosome Browsers, SNPs, and third-party software tools. I will discuss how surname searches, matches in common, notes, and attached family trees can help unlock the confusion of your DNA results.

My strategy to research my DNA match results is:
1. Determine the estimated generation of the common ancestor using the projected relationship of your closest individual matches.
2. Using the surname search tool, enter the surnames of all ancestors at the projected generation of the "common match."
3. When the surname search produces a list of matches, enter the surname in the notes tool for each match on the results list
4. Next, use the shared match tool and select the match with the closest relationship. Then add the surname

to the notes of this set of matches which the previous searches did not identify with a surname. Repeat this step until you have assigned a surname branch to all of your close matches (1st to 3rd cousins).

5. Review the attached family trees for your matches to identify known common ancestors and include this information in the notes.

6. Do further surname searches with the surnames from older generations and continue to add your results to notes for each match.

7. Contact close matches (1st, 2nd, and 3rd) who do not have family trees attached to their DNA account. Using the information, share with them the names of possible common ancestors, and ask them to confirm.

8. Once your contacts have responded and confirmed the common ancestor, share small relevant sections of your family history and ask them also to share what they have, i.e., pictures, copies of documents, and family stories.

The results of the above analysis may point to asking strangers for family information. Approach this request carefully and with sensitivity because you are invading their privacy.

Below is my FTDNA page showing some of my people matches. (I have changed the names to protect their privacy.)

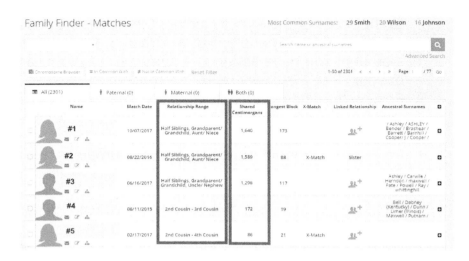

Next to the person's silhouette or picture are the icons of three of the tools: Contact Info, Enter Notes, and the Family Tree. If the icon is blue for the notes or family tree, you have entered information in the note, and the test-taker has attached a family tree. If the icon is black, there is no information in notes and the person has not uploaded a family tree.

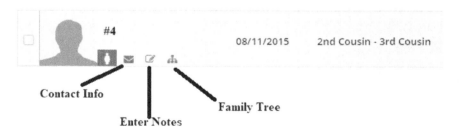

The next columns have the date the results were first posted and then the projected relationship.

The projected relationship may show as a parent, aunt, uncle, or sibling, but usually lists the match as a cousin with a range (1st-2nd, 2nd-3rd, 2nd-4th, etc.) based on the amount of matching DNA. When looking at a family tree, the common ancestor will be some level of a grandparent. Below is a simple conversion that calculates the level of grandparent based on the projected level of cousin relationship.

Formula: X great-grandfather = X+1 cousin
(where X equals the level of great-grandparent)

1st great-grandfather = 2nd cousin
2nd great-grandfather = 3rd cousin
3rd great-grandfather = 4th cousin
4th great-grandfather = 5th cousin

Surname Searches

The next step is to review your matches and determine the level of grandparents in your tree to use for your surname search. I used the surnames at the great-grandparent level because my closest match at the time was the 2nd-3rd cousin.

| | #4 | 08/11/2015 | 2nd Cousin - 3rd Cousin | 172 | 19 |

In the Family Trees shown below the Box indicates great-grandparents

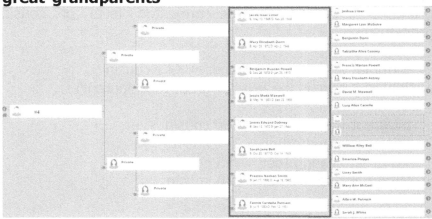

The next step is to identify which branch of your family tree your matches belong. Begin this step by doing a surname search using all of the surnames of my great-grandparents. This exercise will identify the branch where each match belongs.

Below shows the Surname search text box (arrow) on the FTDNA page.

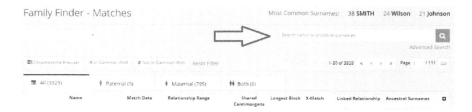

Click on the notes icon and the text box will open. Then, enter the results of each search into the notes box for each match.

Matches in common

After you have entered all of your surnames, review your list of matches and perform the Matches in Common search selecting all close matches that do not yet have a note attached. Select the match by checking the box (circle) on the far left. Then click on the "in common with" (arrow) box. Review each results list to determine which branch this person belongs by opening a few notes where the branch has been identified add that surname to each match that has an empty note. Continue to do this until you have determined the branch for all of your close matches.

Matches "in common with" (Arrow)

Review Family Trees

If you have not uploaded a simple version of your family tree, please do as soon as possible. This version should not be a full version of your tree but should include the names of your direct ancestors. Your tree is an essential communication tool with your matches. Giving them access to the simple version of your tree will help them understand who you are and how they are related. It will encourage them to contact you and share their tree and information with you.

Having a family tree attached to atDNA samples by you and your matches will:
- Allow searching of family trees for surnames that are in your tree
- Will enable you to confirm the generation of the common ancestor to a projected relationship of match

Contact matches without trees

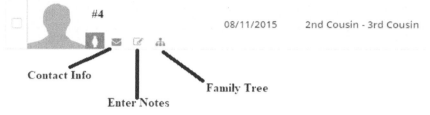

Why contact your matches?
- You need to confirm relationship especially if a family tree not posted
- You need to request an exchange of information
- Contacting your match may help uncover the answer to a mystery

Tips in Contacting Matches
- Upload a complete tree of direct ancestors
- Update your profile
- Send your message from the DNA match page
- Introduce yourself and the purpose of your research
- Be as specific as possible to avoid confusion. Vague messages make it difficult to give a helpful response
- Possibly a list of common ancestors as indicated by the projected relationship
- Do not overwhelm with too much information as this may discourage a reply
- Don't assume the person you are contacting is a genealogist

If they do not respond to your contact, do not stalk them or continue to contact them if they do not respond

Samples of AncestryDNA web pages

On the next page is a sample of AncestryDNA's individual matches page. (I have changed the names due to privacy concerns.)

- Ancestry sorts the results into relationship groups starting with close family, then 1st cousins, 2nd cousins, and then more. The list also shows the projected relationships under the names of each match.
- The arrow points to the amount of matching DNA and the number of segments that have matching DNA.
- The black arrow points to a small icon of a page and will show that you have entered information into a note for that person.
- We can view the family tree, enter information into notes, and do "Matches in Common" searches by clicking on the "View Match" button.
- You can do surname searches by clicking on the Blue "Search Matches" button at the top right.

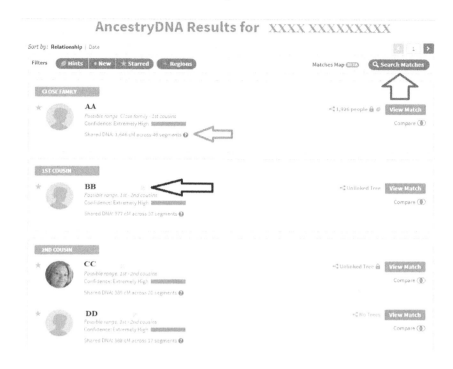

Sample of text boxes to do a "Surname Search."
Note that you can search for surnames and birth locations

Below is a sample of the "View Match" page for the individual GG. It shows a small tree and gives you access to more functions:

- Read and enter notes (see Box) which includes information from notes previously or empty text box where you can enter your note. If you click on the pencil icon, you can edit a previous note. Clicking on the trash can icon will delete the note.
- The bottom section shows the tree for the person.
- The small black toolbar in the center of the page includes a bottom that will do a "Shared Matches" search.
- The green button in the upper right allows you to contact the person who submitted the sample.

Sample of page "View Match."

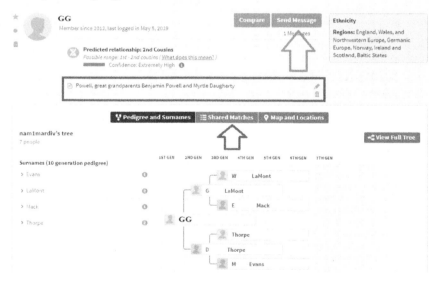

Examples of MyHeritageDNA Pages

Below and on the next two pages are examples of the DNA results pages on MyHeritageDNA. The page below shows the first two of my matches. I have changed the names to JJ and ML. The second column next to their names indicates the projected relationship. The third column lists the amount of shared DNA (both as a percentage and centimorgans), the number of shared segments, and the longest segment. For more information about your match to a specific person, click on the "Review DNA Match" button.

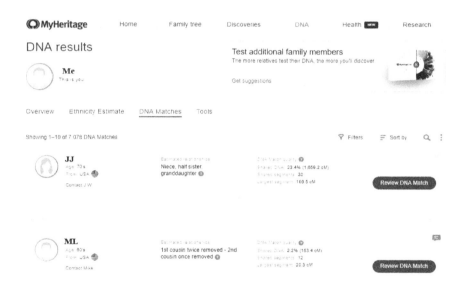

Below and on the next page are examples of the information shown on the "Review DNA Match" page. The section shown below lists the first two "Matches in Common" I have with ML. The far-right indicates my projected relationship with the match, and the far-left column indicates the project relationship of ML to the match. The center section lists the amount of matching DNA with the match. Scroll down the webpage for more information about my match with ML.

Review DNA Match

Scrolling down the page, we next see the shared ethnicities I have with ML. MyHeritageDNA shows this as percentages and also balloons on a map. Below the shared ethnicities are the chromosome browser showing the shared DNA segments between me and my match ML.

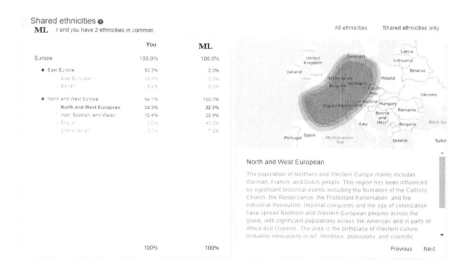

AncestryDNA - Two More Tools
AncestryDNA has two tools not offered by the other DNA testing companies: **Genetic Communities and ThruLines.** I have found both tools helpful but with limitations.

Genetic Community (Ancestry only)
Below are two web pages from my AncestryDNA's Genetic Communities results. The first page shows balloons in Europe, which depict the origins of the population for the genetic community. The next page shows the migration from Europe to an area in America. Both pages gave me insights that helped me to understand my DNA results better. Knowing the approximate area where my ancestors left gave me insight on how to use the DNA matches, I saw in my results. The images did not give me specific information but gave me clues on where to look for more details.

European Origins of Genetic Community

Migration of Genetic Community

ThruLines (AncestryDNA only)

ThruLines has excellent features and a potential to be a useful tool, but it has limitations that need to be recognized. It uses your family tree and the family trees from your DNA matches to point to common ancestors. It shows you a large family tree faster than building a family tree on Ancestry.com, and it may seem like magic. However, we need to be careful about how we use the information because of the possible inaccuracy of the family trees and the methods AncestryDNA uses to project your unknown ancestors. By using the DNA matches to estimated relationships, ThruLines has more potential to project correct ancestors than the hints attached to your family trees. However, care must be taken to verify all new relationships because the family trees of your DNA matches may be wrong, and ThruLines may be suggesting false information. Also, Ancestry may be using many wrong family trees that have been stitched together and may contain erroneous information that has been passed along for many generations. ThruLines has value only when we use it within its limitations. Use it for the clues but always verify the relationships.

On the next page are images of two portions of my Thrulines tree. The first image shows my parents and grandparents. I have blocked off their names. The second image shows a part of my 4th Great-grandparents. The second image shows two types of relationships. The top line is some of the relationships recommended by AncestryDNA from the trees of my DNA matches, and the second line is from my family tree. Although the suggested relationships seem to appear magically to fill out our family trees, they still need to be verified by traditional methods and if possible, with conventional genealogical sources.

The final image on the next two pages shows my relationship through a common ancestor Francis Powell to four of my DNA matches. I have blocked out their names for privacy. I was able to see this last image by clicking on Francis in my ThruLines tree. This final image is helpful because it gives me specific information to mention when I contact my matches and ask to exchange information.

Beginning of my ThruLine Tree

A portion of my 4th Great-grandparents

ThruLines Tree showing Frances Powell as my Common Ancestor to some of my DNA Matches

Who has the Tools
- Surname searches (All four major companies)
- Shared Matches (Ancestry, FamilytreeDNA, 23andMe, & MyHeritageDNA)
- Notes for matches (Ancestry, FamilytreeDNA, & MyHeritageDNA)
- Family Trees (all but 23andMe)
- Genetic Communities (Ancestry only)
- ThruLines (AncestryDNA only)
- Contact Matches (All four major companies)

Chapter Three will cover a case study showing how to use the tools to make sense of surprise results by find finding a biological father using the above DNA tools and traditional genealogical resources and skills. No family stories were available to give clues.

Chapter Three - Case Study: Mystery DNA & Dark Secrets

Do you have unexplained ethnicity in your DNA results? Mystery DNA or unexplained ethnicity is frustrating and creates a challenge to understand. This chapter examines the mystery DNA results for an individual and discusses the steps used to find their previously unknown biological father.

The chart shown below lists the ethnic results for Sam as projected by the four major DNA testing companies: AncestryDNA, Family Tree DNA, My Heritage, and 23andMe. The first box highlights a range of English/Irish DNA from 13% to 40% where traditional genealogical documents for Sam indicates there should be no English/Irish DNA. Sam also submitted a Y-DNA sample, and the results pointed to German roots from the Rhine River area instead of the expected Jewish roots in Hungary. So, both autosomal and Y-DNA tests produced unexplained DNA results for Sam.

Sam's Mystery DNA (2018)

Ethnic Group	Ancestry	Familytree	MyHeritage	23andMe	Research
English/Irish	40%	36%	16%	13%	0%
Europe East	35%	63%	50%	See below	See below
Polish				30%	50%
Hungarian					25%
Gypsy					12.5%
Jewish					12.5%
Europe West	14%		34%	10%	0%
Scandinavia	9%			5%	0%
Other	2%	1%		1%	
Broadly Europe				9%	
Broadly NW Europe				31%	
Broadly Southern Europe				1%	
Total	100%	100%	100%	100%	100%

Do other family members have Sam's mystery DNA? Sam asked other family members to submit DNA samples[3].

- Don, a 1st cousin, and Jeff, a 2nd cousin, submitted Y-DNA samples which did not match with Sam's sample but did match with each other. Their sample also matches with an individual whose ancestor was Jewish and was born in the area in Hungary where Sam's paternal great-grandfather was born.
- Lynn, a second cousin, submitted an autosomal sample, and she did not match with Sam, and she was not Sam's 1s cousin. Her results included 24% Jewish ethnicity, which was close to the expected levels for her relationship with her grandfather.
- Don, Jeff, and Lynn were Sam's cousin from his father's side of the family, and their DNA confirmed their relationships in the family tree generated from documents.
- Sam's sister, Jan, submitted an autosomal sample and she matched with Lynn as a 2nd cousin, but FTDNA projected her relationship with Sam as a half-sister.

The results from the DNA tests identified the origins of Sam's mystery DNA. The mystery came from an unknown biological father who was not the father listed on his birth certificate. Sam and Jan did not have the same father, but DNA confirms they had the same mother. Sam was not adopted but the product of a previously unknown event.

Who was Sam's biological father? What clues were available? There seemed to be no one to give Sam any information since his mother, grandparents, and his mother's close friends were no longer alive.

---

[3] Most of the names mentioned in this chapter has been changed to protect the privacy of the individuals

Using clues from his DNA results and traditional genealogical skills and sources, Sam found his biological father. A miracle may have occurred, but the name of his father did not magically appear. Sam found the identity through genealogical research using his DNA results and traditional sources.

What clues did Sam have?
- His paternal immigrant came from the Rhine River area in Germany.
- His Y-DNA gave Wertemberger as his paternal surname.
- His biological father was in central Illinois in 1946.

What sources were available?
- Family trees from Sam's DNA matches on AncestryDNA and FTDNA
- The U.S. Federal Census
- The 1946 city directory for the town where Sam was born
- Online Public Family Trees from Ancestry.com

Sam's first step in his search for his biological father was to use his DNA matches to identify surnames who were part of his new family. His closest match was ML on Family Tree DNA and who was a second or third cousin. Below is shown a screen print of ML's listing in Sam's Family Tree DNA match list.

| ML | | 08/11/2015 | 2nd Cousin - 3rd Cousin | 172 | 19 |

ML did not attach a family tree to his DNA results, but Sam contacted ML through FTDNA to request a copy of ML's family tree. The family tree gave Sam a list of surnames to enter into the Surname Search box to find which set of great-grandparents or 2nd great-grandparents were the common ancestors for Sam and ML.

The next step was to enter the surnames from the family tree. First, all of the surnames for the great-grandparents and then the 2nd great-grandparents if needed. Then review the matches. This exercise identified a pair of great-grandparents who were common ancestors of Sam and ML.

In the Family Trees shown below the Box indicates great-grandparents

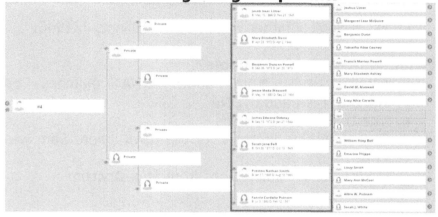

Sam's search pointed to Benjamin Powell and Jessie Maxwell as his new great-grandparents and a common ancestor with ML.

Please note that projecting Benjamin and Jessie as Sam's great-grandparents are contingent on Sam conducting further research and identifying his biological father as their descendant. This guideline is correct for all projected relationships in Sam's search for his biological father.

Sam searched Benjamin and Jessie in U.S. Federal Census records and online family trees and determined that he had found the English/Irish family that his DNA ethnicity results identified, but he had not found the name of his biological father.

Sam's Y-DNA test projected that Sam's new family name began with the letter W and his paternal left Germany. These facts predicted Benjamin and Jessie as Sam's maternal great-grandparents because their family name began with "P" and their roots were English and Irish. One of their daughters had to be Sam's grandmother and the father of his biological father.

The family trees and the 1910 Census indicated Benjamin and Jessie had six children: three sons and three daughters. Their daughter Mary was the grandmother of ML and lived in central Illinois near Sam's birthplace. Their daughter Margaret married and moved to Michigan and did not have a son who could be Sam's father. Their daughter Lula married and moved to the town where Sam was born. She married Roy Whitehead.

Were Roy and Lula the parents of Sam's biological father?

- Their surname began with "W."
- Roy's paternal family tree traced back to an immigrant who had unknown origins but may have left Germany. The source for this information was the online trees on Ancestry.com
- The 1930 and 1940 census records and 1946 city directories indicate that Roy and Lula lived in Sam's birthplace.
- The 1930 and 1940 census records listed that Roy and Lula had four sons who were the right ages to be Sam's father.
- None of their sons were alive when Sam identified them as his possible biological father.

Sam's next step was to establish contact with a descendant of one of the four sons to ask them to volunteer to submit an autosomal DNA test sample. Luckily, Sam found a granddaughter of one of the sons on Facebook and sent her a private message asking her or her husband to call him. She nervously did call Sam and listened to his request and explanation. She passed the information along to her father, who had his older brother give Sam a call to discuss the DNA test. Sam ordered Y-DNA and Autosomal test kits. Note the Y-DNA test was needed to confirm the origin of the Whitehead family was from the Rhine River area in Germany. The results of both the Y-DNA and atDNA tests match with Sam. The results of the Y-DNA test confirmed the Whitehead family originated in the Rhine River area in Germany and the atDNA test results identified Sam's biological father. The results also determined that Sam had two new half-brothers and a new half-sister.

Below shows the first four matches Sam's new FTDNA matches page. Person #1 is Sam's new sister, #2 is Sam's sister, #3 is Sam's new older brother, and #4 is Sam's 2nd cousin ML.

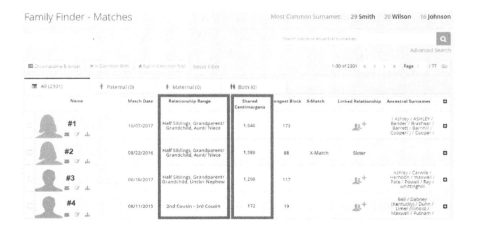

Sam found his biological father and also found three new siblings. This discovery allowed him to research his new family roots and write a new family history for his grandchildren.

Sam's success was not magic. He used the basic tools that were available from the testing companies to find clues and used his genealogical skills to put his puzzle together.

- He contacted a projected cousin and obtained a copy of the cousin's family tree.
- Using his cousin's family tree, Sam did surname searches of his DNA matches to identify possible great-grandparents.
- He used notes and "Matches in Common" to organize his matches.
- He used census records and City directories to identify possible family members who were living in his birthplace when he was born.
- He used online family trees to eliminate families from his list and identify possible families.
- Using all of these sources, he narrowed his list to one possible family.
- He searched the internet and found a way to contact a possible family member in a sensitive and private method.
- He asked a possible family member to take DNA tests.
- He used Y-DNA and autosomal test samples to produce more matches to identify and confirm the name of his biological father.

It was not magic, but the use of DNA results combined with traditional genealogical sources and methods.

Chapter Four - Emotional Concerns about DNA Test Results

If your DNA results do not make sense, ask yourself these questions before you try to uncover the answers:
- Do you need to know the answer?
- Are you prepared to deal with a dark secret that may upset the family?
- What will you do with the information once you know the answer?

Be prepared for bad news and dark secrets!

Finding answers to your DNA test results can change known relationships by uncovering the existence of previously unknown biological parents. You may immediately think of adoption as the cause for unknown parents, but researchers have also identified unwed mothers and infidelity as significant sources of DNA surprises. Another frequent reason for unknown parents would be the remarriage of a spouse after the other spouse dies young, leaving children. The new relationships may affect your parents, grandparents, or with earlier generations. Please remember, genealogists must respect the privacy of family members when uncovering "secrets" in documents and now DNA testing makes privacy issues even more critical because of the nature of the information revealed.

Suddenly finding out we have an unknown biological parent or grandparent in our family history will probably cause immediate emotional issues.

- If they were not due to adoption, how did it occur?
- How can I find the name of my unknown parent or ancestor?
- Should I find out?

The search for the answers will be challenging if the problem was in an older generation because the documents probably do not exist, and people who knew may be dead.

Autosomal test results usually give a list of second and third cousins. Some of these we may know, or in many cases, they belong to branches that your family has lost contact. We should be able to find the common ancestor for most of these relationships, but some will be challenging because of the lack of paperwork, or the DNA may have found an unexpected relationship.

If previously unknown first cousins or half-siblings appear in your results, your world will change dramatically. These new relationships may be a total surprise to all family members but also may be a secret and not talked about by older family members. However, the relationship will be difficult to document on paper and maybe problematic to be understood by other family members. Listen for relatives who strongly oppose taking a DNA because they may know the reason for the unexplained relationship.

When we took our DNA tests, most of us did not understand all of the ramifications that the results may show. We were only looking for information either to: identify our ethnic heritage or extend our family history stories by meeting other relatives. In some cases, test-takers were looking to confirm family stories such as native American ethnicity. We never understood that the results might disrupt our long-held relationships. If you understood the risk, would you still have taken the test? Should we hide from the possibility of finding problematic information by not taking a test or should we seek accuracy in the family history that we want to pass along to our future generations? I do know the answer for you. Only you can answer this question for your family history.

Test-takers need to be prepared to handle the discovery of shocking information about previously unknown relationships that will disrupt families from going forward. Your parent or other family members kept this secret for a reason and felt that it would die with them. DNA has invalidated that strategy.

If you uncover a dark secret such as previously unknown illegitimate children, ask yourself how each of your family members will react? Ask yourself how will telling your family members the details of a dark family secret affect your relationship with them? Do you need to reveal the secret? Can you tell some affected family members but not everyone?

If we helped a friend or relative take a DNA, what does our obligation to them on understanding the test results? Did they ask you for help with the test, or did you ask the relative to take the test? If you see that their results may lead to a dark secret, do you have a responsibility to tell them? No laws or standards are requiring a specific response, but in most cases, I believe the answer is yes, but please be sensitive and be prepared for an emotional reaction.

Adoptees are a large group of people who are using DNA testing to find their biological parents, and this search can lead to many difficult ethical issues. There are state laws that protect against revealing information in the adoption documents. The laws are meant to protect the information about the adoptee, the biological parents, and the adoptive parents. However, DNA testing is a way to circumvent these restrictions. DNA test results can provide clues and a path for adoptees to find their biological parents. Once the adoptee finds the names, should the rights of the adoptee prevail over the rights of the biological parents or the adoptive parents? Adoption information presents us with a minefield of potential ethical issues created by using DNA test results. Everyone should have the right to their data, but the laws are meant to protect all three groups.

Two other DNA-related issues that are prevalent:
1. Making sure test samples are submitted by the test-taker or with their permission. Testing companies have recently changed their submission procedure to ensure the test-taker provided the sample, and they have access to the information.
2. Genealogists need to restrict sharing the names and profile information of their matches publicly.

Before you take a DNA test, try to understand the possible outcomes of a DNA test. After you submit your sample, be prepared for unexpected issues. Once you have your results, handle problematic information responsibly by responding discreetly.

Be sensitive to your family members. Please consider that some family members do not have to know, but some family members need to know. Everyone will react differently and be careful with who you tell and how you say it.

The only way to prevent the disclosure of problematic genealogical information is to avoid all genealogical research and DNA testing.

Lettin' the cat outta the bag is a whole lot easier 'n puttin' it back in.

by Will Rogers

Chapter Five - Last Thoughts

I have only talked about the basic tools because these tools can answer most of our questions about our DNA results. DNA testing companies and third-party companies offer more tools that are useful in analyzing DNA results. I have not needed to use these tools, but other genealogists have found them helpful when analyzing complicate relationships or family groupings. However, we need an understanding of the science of DNA testing and the use of scientific analysis to effectively use these advanced tools.

Here are four of the advanced tools:
- Chromosome browsers which are available at FTDNA, 23andMe, and MyHeritageDNA and allows us to see which DNA segment we have in common with each match.
- DNA Painter is a website that you can use to help you map your chromosome browser segments as compared to your matches. It allows you to visualize and make notes on your DNA matches. It helps sort through your matches and assign them to different batches of your family tree by coloring coding your segments. The app sounds easy to use, but we will need to be familiar with the chromosome browser to benefit from DNA Painter fully.
- Auto clustering is a third-party tool that groups your matches in related clusters into a graph and analysis of the members of each group should help you understand how you are related to each group. The application is one of the tools that are available with MyHeritageDNA, and we can also use it from the Autoclustering website by allowing access to your DNA results from FTDNA, AncestryDNA, and

23andMe.[4] This tool arranges your matches into clusters to give a visible grouping of your matches.

---

[4]Visit the Genetic Affairs website to find out more about using Autoclustering at https://dna-explained.com/2018/12/04/autoclustering-by-genetic-affairs/

- GEDMatch.com is a website created to let DNA test-takers compare their results with more samples from other people by allowing the upload of raw data from FTDNA, 23andMe, and AncestryDNA to their platform which created one large file of DNA data. The chromosome browser is one of the tools available on this website, and it will find matches with other individuals. However, GEDMatch does not offer surname searches, matches-in-common, attaching family trees, and notes.

The use of DNA in genealogy will continue to grow. The ethnic results will become more accurate, and the individual matches will become easier to interpret.

Genealogy is an addiction, and analyzing DNA results can quickly add to this addiction. Before you devote significant amounts of time analyzing all of your DNA results, consider the following:

- Do you need to identify your common ancestor with all of your DNA matches?
- What information can 4th and 5th cousins add to your family history?
- Watch out for "rabbit holes."
- Do not let the time you spend analyzing your DNA overwhelm your other genealogical areas of research.
- You will have more success by using DNA along with your other tools.

DNA is a new and powerful tool, but genealogy researchers need to remember it is just one tool in their toolbox. They need to remember to use all of their weapons and make their research more powerful.

Also, remember that genealogy research is always changing and genealogists must never stop their education. They must stay on top of the latest developments in genealogical research, which also includes advancements in DNA testing and analysis.

Why do you want to take a DNA test?
  Do you want to:
- Know more about their origins or ethnicity?
- Know Medical information?
- Exchange information?
- Prove or disprove your family oral history?
- Test family relationship theories?
- Know more about what the results would show?

However, Remember:

If your DNA results do not make sense, what will you do with the information once you solve the mystery?

Chapter Five - Last Thoughts

Index

T

ThruLines, 40

Y

Y-DNA, 2, 5, 7, 49, 51

The Author

Stephen Szabados is a lecturer and author who has given numerous programs to genealogy groups and libraries. He has a Bachelor of Science degree from the University of Illinois and an MBA from Northern Illinois University. He is the author of over ten genealogy books and over fifteen family histories. He is also a contributing editor for the Polish American Journal. He is a member of Polish Genealogical Society of America, Northwest Suburban Genealogy Society, Illinois Genealogy Society and a genealogy volunteer at his local library. He has a passion for sharing his love of family history, and his courses cover the methods that he has found successful in his twenty years of research experience.

Other Books by the Stephen Szabados

Print Books (all books are available on Amazon.com, click on the price to access)

Basic Genealogy: Saving Your Family History
Find your roots! Start your search now. This book reviews a process that will help everyone start their research, and it gives hints that will make your research successful.
Price: $9.99

Basic Genealogy and Beyond: Easy steps to find your Family History and tips to break down Brick Walls
This book goes beyond the great tips I covered in "Basic Genealogy" and gives many additional methods and sources to find more information to help create a wonderful family history of your ancestors. My new book includes new material that covers search tips, organization, an outline of steps to find where your European immigrants left, and the basics of using DNA testing in genealogy.
Price: $17.99

Write Your Family History: Easy Steps to Organize, Save and Share
Writing a family history can seem to be a very challenging project for many people. However, organizing your research into a format that is easily read by your family is a must. The methods discussed in this book will show the reader a simple format that will make this task much more manageable.
Price: $17.99

Finding Grandma's European Ancestors: Revised 2016

Want to find your European roots? This book gives you easy steps to find where your ancestors left and tips on where to find the European records of your ancestors. Most European countries are covered.
Price: $19.99

Polish Genealogy: Four Steps to Success

This book gives the researcher the tools needed to research their Polish ancestors and find possible answers to the origins of their Polish heritage. The book outlines a simple process that will identify where your ancestors were born and where to find their Polish records.
Price: $19.99

Polish Immigration to America: When, Where, Why and How

When did your Polish ancestors immigrate, where did they leave, why did they leave, how did they get here? These are questions we all hope to find the answers. This book discusses the history of Poland and gives some insights into possible answers to the questions about your ancestors' immigration.
Price: $17.99

Find Your Czech and Slovak Ancestors

This book is a great source to find the Czech and Slovak records for your ancestors. The book outlines a simple process that will identify where your ancestors were born and where to find their European records.
Price: $19.99

Print and eBooks

My Polish Grandmother: from Tragedy in Poland to her Rose Garden in America

The story of Anna's life is different from many stories of immigrants because it is told from the perspective of a woman. She suffered through tragedies in her life in Poland but found the strength to build a new life in the U. S.

Print book Price: $14.99
eBook Price: $7.99

Memories of Dziadka

This book is about the life of a Polish immigrant – his early life in Poland, his travel to America and his life in Illinois. I also try to describe why his simple life was important to all of us.

Print book Price: $17.99
eBook Price: $7.99

eBooks

Hints for Translating Polish Genealogical Records

A quick reference guide to help the researcher translate the Polish genealogical records of their ancestors.

eBook Price: $2.99

Deciphering the 1790-1840 U.S. Census Records: Two case studies

Census records are a snapshot of your family and finding all of these records is an important task in researching your family history. This book reviews two case studies that will give you hints on how to decipher the early U.S census, which is challenging to use because they list only the head of the household.

eBook Price: $0.99

Quick Reference to U.S. Census Records: a snapshot of the past

Census records are a snapshot of your family at the time the census was taken and contain a wealth of information that can be used the lives of your family. This book explains the information that is included in the census records and how they can be used in your family histories. The book also points to where these records can be found and also includes some search tips.

eBook Price: $2.99

Made in United States
North Haven, CT
06 March 2023

33687629R00054